WAKE UP AMERICA!!

Views of a hard-working, red-blooded, flag-waving,
right-thinking regular American

**Earl Pitts, American
with Gary Burbank & Tim Mizak**

ISBN: 149427969X
ISBN-13: 978-1494279691

DEDICATION

Pearl, Carol and Darlene - the women that have put up with us all these years.

JD, Rob, Jim, Kel, and Len, for their continued work at the Duck Inn.

Rocco, Nathan and Bill for opening new doors and pushing us through them.

The hundreds of radio stations and thousands of loyal fans who listen every day to find out what makes me sick.

And finally, to Dub and Junior Meeker - for making me look like a genius in comparison.

Pitts Off!

CONTENTS

CHAPTER ONE
REAL AMERICAN MEN

Earl Pitts

Crying Movies

You know what makes me sick? You know what makes me so angry I just wanna go rent one a' them Merl Streep movies for tonight... take it home... an' shoot it!?!?

Yeah — here's to the further wussification of the American male. An' this is ticking me off to no end. Y'all seen where some hanky-blowing twit on the computer somewhere came up with a new list... the Top Twenty-Five movies that make men cry?

Yeah — they say these are the top movies...guaranteed to make men all weepy an' stupid. The number one biggest cry-baby pictures for men – is *Field a' Dreams*... followed by *Old Yeller, Brian's Song, Braveheart* an' *Rudy.*

Yeah — we got a name for men that cry when they watch pictures. We call'em... **women**!!!

Number one – I ain't never cried watching no stupid picture. Number two – if I ever did... I sure as hell wouldn't admit it. An' number three – I'd dive head-first into a wood-chipper before I ever came up with a list a' pictures that made me cry!

Only two times a man should ever cry in his life... if he takes a hard liner to the crotch... or if he ever gets the opportunity to hear Lee Greenwood sing "Proud to be a' American"... live in person.

Wake Up America!!!

I mean they even come up with a list. What's so weepy cry-baby sad about these movies? Field a' Dreams? Some sod-busting idiot digs up his corn field an' builds a ball diamond. That ain't sad – that's stupid. The price a' corn these days... it's his old lady should be crying... not me!

An' guys cry at Old Yeller? They do? What in the Sam Hill? It's like y'all never had to shoot a dog before! An' okay – I did get a little misty-eyed at Brian's Song. But that's only because three-quarters a' the way through... I suddenly realized that was two hours of my life... I was never gonna get back...

Wake up, America. If y'all ever see Earl Pitts at the picture show... an' it looks like I'm crying... it's only because I just spent fifteen bucks on popcorn an' a coke. Lord – I'll be crying like a baby. I'm Earl Pitts, American. Pitts Off!

Earl Pitts

Junkyards

You know what makes me sick? You know what makes me so mad I just wanna do my part to help turn around the auto industry... by going to Detroit... an' volunteering to be a crash-test dummy?

Yeah – the other day... I was helping my buddy, Dub Meeker with his truck. His power steering pump was shot. You could still drive it... as long as the only direction you went ... was straight.

So we done what real men do. We went to the junkyard. An' let me tell you something... the further wussification of America has hit the junk business. Yeah – first off... they ain't even called "junkyards" no more. They are now "auto recyclers". They've even got everything on computer. I mean, we told this old dude what we needed... he starts to pecking on some computer terminal like he was a NASA scientist. Then he said he'd text message some kid in the yard... an' they'd find it right off.

What the hell happened? I remember when junkyards were *junkyards*. You'd walk into some smoky office that smelled like gasoline, brake-fluid, anti-freeze an' tuna. There'd be a girly calendar on the wall. It'd be the wrong month... a' the wrong year... Yeah – but it'd be the right woman.

Wake Up America!!!

There'd be a couch over to one side... with a red stain on it. Could be transmission fluid... could be blood. Cause in the junk business... both would be spilled liberally.

An' most important... you showed up with your own tools. Some crotchety old fart would scratch his head a couple times... an' then somehow magically remember where a half-way decent '92 F-150 was hiding... with most of its parts still workable. An' then he'd send you off into the graveyard of twisted metal. You'd come back three hours later... with the part you needed... an' seven more parts you figured looked promising. Just in case.

That, my friends... was a junkyard. Run by scary people... protected by scary dogs... An visited by scary rednecks. We're still here – where did everybody else go?

Wake up, America. He did have a dog, though. A poodle he kept calling "Jimmy". Yeah – I've been in junkyards that had rats bigger than Jimmy. I think I'm gonna be sick! I'm Earl Pitts, American. Pitts Off!

Earl Pitts

Man Eyeballs

You know what makes me sick? You know what makes me so mad I just wanna chug embalming fluid...?

Yeah – last week another one of the guys down at the plant keeled over an' died. Not at work... he was at home when he bought the farm. Which – oddly enough... is a farm. His name was Eddie.

So anyways - me and my buddy Dub Meeker went down to the funeral home – to pay our respects. An' things were going pretty much like you'd expect. The widow looked shell-shocked. A' lot a people were crying An' a bunch of other people were standing around looking like they had just lost their best friend. Which – oddly enough – is exactly what had just happened.

Anyways... I'm going up there to comfort the widow with a couple a' funny Eddie stories... when I noticed this beautiful young lady setting over to the side. I mean – she was wearing a respectful black dress – but I think she left the bottom of the dang thing at home. An' I don't know what the rules are about burying dead people... an' cleavage... but she was pushing the envelope. If you know what I mean?

So Dub sees me staring... an' he goes, "'Earl, cut that out! It ain't right to be leering at the ladies at a funeral."

Wake Up America!!!

So folks... let me enlighten y'all about what I like to call – your real man eyeball nature.   An' this is the deal. Your eyeballs don't care where the rest of you is... man eyeballs are gonna do what man eyeballs do. Hunt for good looking women.

Tell me I ain't telling the god's honest truth men. How many of y'all been in the doctor's office... he's like straightening out your broken leg or something ... an' you're looking down the nurse's scrubs when she bends over to take your temperature? Right before you pass out from the pain.

Hey – you could be on trial for bank-robbery... extortion... racketeering... and you're gonna be setting at the defense table... staring at the stenographer... if she's pretty. It ain't us, ladies... it's our real man eyeball nature.

Wake up, America.   My ol' lady wants to know how come I always want to set up front in church. I tell her I need to get closer to heaven. What she don't know is heaven is "the rack" on that new organist. It's not me – it's my eyeballs. I'm Earl Pitts, American. Pitts Off.

Earl Pitts

Moving Friends

You know what makes me sick? You know what makes me so mad I just wanna pick the ticks off a stray dog... with my teeth??

Ya'll know I love my truck, right? Any real man loves a real truck — and not one a' those sissy baby-trucks... but a real man-size truck. That being said... there is a downside to owning a real man-size truck. All your friends figure you're in the moving business.

Like last weekend... Junior Meeker asked me if I'd help him move. It's like the third time he's moved in the last four years. Lord, I can't figure out if the boy's a deadbeat ... or a fugitive.

Now — I can't complain too much... on account of him letting me use his bass boat... but I do have some rules on helping people move.

Rule number one, you buy the beer. **Rule number two**, you buy the pizza. **Rule number three,** when we're done with the pizza... you go buy some more beer.

Now — a very important rule... is **rule number four**. By the time I get to your place... you better have got all your crap boxed up an' ready to haul. Cause I ain't lifting no dang furniture while you're setting there sorting through your DVD collection. I ain't popping no groin muscles while you're still writing "kitchen" on the side a' boxes with a magic marker. Bull puckey on that!!

Rule number five... if you're gonna wear one a' them weight-lifter belts an' them gloves with the fingers cut off... you better be toting more than a table lamp, Sampson. No sir... you better have a couch tucked up under one arm... an' a dresser under the other if you're gonna wear that nonsense.

Rule number six... if I happen to drop a box an' you hear a bunch of stuff break inside... it's your own fault. You're the one that bought the greasy pizza... an' got me half loaded on beer. What did you expect?

Rule number seven... when we're carrying furniture...I am *not* the one walking backwards. You're the one that knows where all the funny places are in the yard.

Wake up, America. **Rule number eight**... I'm only making two trips... so keep piling it in the pick-up. As long as we clear the underpasses... we'll be fine. I'm Earl Pitts, American. Pitts Off!!!

Canteens

You know what makes me sick? You know what makes me so mad I just wanna hike cross country... on my hands an' knees?

You know – I just saw something the other day... it just struck me as wrong. Me an' my old lady went down to the park... to walk around the lake. You know... we're getting exercise now.

First off... if you actually work for a living... doing honest manual labor... you don't need no exercising. Because – correct me if I'm wrong, gentlemen – *life*... is a work out.

Well – anyway... that fact ain't gonna take the lard of my old lady's keester – so we were down there doing laps. An' all these yuppie bone-heads were down there... power-walking an' jogging... with those little wires sticking out of their fool heads. And I couldn't help but notice... they were all carrying plastic bottles a' water.

And you know what struck me? What the hell ever happened to a canteen?

I don't remember John Wayne ever crossing no desert... with no dang water bottle. I don't remember our GI's fighting Nazism... and Communism... with no water bottles. I don't remember Lewis an' Clark discovering

Wake Up America!!!

the Pacific Ocean with an Indian chick... and two water bottles!!

No sir –they all had canteens. An' if a canteen was good enough to build America... it's good enough for some Yuppie panty-waist in stretch pants.

I mean – can a water bottle deflect a bullet when you're surrounded by Indians? I don't think so.

An' I'll tell you another thing... that's how you can tell a real man these days. A real man – actually *has* a canteen. He might not know where it is anymore... but he could dig it up... if he was desperate. It's probably in the garage somewhere... an' it might still have 30-year old Kool-aid in it from a backyard campout in 1980... but he's got one, gol' darn it!! Somewhere...

Wake up, America! Next time you're running a 5k... or one a' those marathons races an' you pass the people handing out water. Say no thank you... I brought my canteen. I'm Earl Pitts. Pitts off!

Man Shoes

You know what makes me sick? You know what makes me so mad I just wanna eat a big bowl a' succotash... made with the corns off my big toe?

Yeah – the other night I was down at the Duck Inn... beer tending... twistin' long-necks a' keepin' the riff-raff quiet. An' then these guys come in there... I hear this flap-flap-flap. I swear to God... they came in there... wearing those flip-flop sandal shoes.

What is this world coming to when somebody wearing those kind of shoes... come walking into my kind of bar? Then I look around... an' half the guys in there were wearing sandals... flip-flops... or those dang circus freak Croc shoes.

Far as I'm concerned... only one *real* man ever worn sandals. An' he used'em to walk on water. So if you can't... you shouldn't.

A real man only needs three pairs a' shoes. Type number one – your work boot. Those are for a man that makes a living on his feet. Could be cowboy boots... could be steel-toed Red Wings. But whatever they are, they're gonna weigh three pounds more when you take them off at the end of the day than when you put them on. Cause they're gonna be full a' sweat. An' they're gonna smell like a cheese an' pickle sandwich left in the sun too long. That's the smell of hard-working

Wake Up America!!!

America right there!

Type number two real man footwear - would be Sunday go-to-church shoes. Now – you'll be wearing these bad boys at most - one to two hours a week... an' maybe to the occasional wedding or funeral, so they should last you a couple decades. I mean – my church shoes now... are the same shoes I wore to my senior prom.

Type number three - yard shoes. These is the shoes you wear in the yard... hanging at the bar... vacation... every place but church an' work. These are usually sneakers. You buy a new pair about every five years. So every five years you get to complain about how much sneakers cost. And how Michael Jordan is a thief...

That's the whole list people... an' I don't see sandals or flip-flops or giant rubber clown shoes on there, nowhere...

Wake up, America. An' in case you forget the list... here's a simple way to remember ... nobody wants to look at man toes. Yikes!!! Those little piggies look like little sausages... holding up shields. I'm Earl Pitts, American. Pitts Off.

Earl Pitts

Man Grilling

You know what makes me sick? You know what makes me so mad I just wanna shish-ka-bob a cat?

Yeah – I thought it was high time we quit belly-aching and whining about the economy the idiots in Washington... and whatever weird disease is putting us on the toilet... and the general orneriness of this year...

Let's take a break from all the bad crap... an' talk about the great American tradition... the backyard barbecue. Just remember... they can take our money... they can take our spirit. But they can't take away our grills. Although they could be working on that, too.

There ain't nothing better on this earth than the sound of a big slab of anything dripping grease on a bed a' hot coals.... t-ssss, t-ssss... man, you can almost taste it.

Backyard barbecue is what real Americans do. And I ain't talking about those loser metro-sexual, do-it-yourself snobs with some pansy gas grill, on some fancy hard-wood deck, in freaking suburbia somewhere... You know who I'm talking 'bout, right? Throws a couple burgers on some $500-dollar grill with more knobs and switches than the space shuttle... an' right away thinks he's the Iron Chef.

That's bull puckey! Your Real American is scrapping two-inches of petrified burger bits off a rusty grill... that sat outside all winter. He's probably got to scoop out a squirrel nest in there. Fires that bad boy up... just to burn off the grease from last year. For the first fifteen or twenty minutes – it smells like he's burning a tire... Now – *that's a backyard barbecue.*

An' don't get me wrong... I ain't got nothing against them fancy-butt yuppie gas grills. You can use'em if you got'em. But then again... you can also wear a dress if you run out of pants!! Get my point?!

Here's another thing... I was watching that food channel one time... an' some idiot was on there... grilling *vegetables.* That right there... is a waste of good heat. Unless it's some sweet corn on the cob... an' that ain't in season yet. So forget it!

Wake up, America! Dogs, burgers, sausages... steaks... chicken... beef... an' 21 different types a' pork... that's all you need. And plenty of lighter fluid. And maybe a fire extinguisher. I'm Earl Pitts, American. Pitts Off!!

Earl Pitts

Spicy Food

You know what makes me sick? You know what makes me so angry I just wanna roll around naked in a room full of broken glass... an' then set in a hot tub filled with Tabasco sauce...???

I was listening to these boneheads the other day... an' they were talking 'bout some story 'bout some genius in England somewhere. Anyways - this idiot killed himself by making his chili too spicy. Yeah – he was having a chili cook-off with a friend... to see who could make the hottest chili. When he tasted some of his own creation... he keeled over dead.

Man, that must have been some good stuff.

Now - I bring up this story... cause I can guaran-dang-tee you 75% a' the men that hear that story are thinking... "I could have ate that..."

See the thing is... real men love hot, spicy food. Not your wussy, metro-sexual, yuppie girly-men, mind you... but real men. The hotter – the better – am I right gentlemen? But I will give you this... I would stop short of food so hot it could kill me. I might taste it a little... though.

An' your women – well – they just don't get it. Women don't seem to appreciate food with names like

Wake Up America!!!

"atomic", "five-alarm" or "butt-burner"... or "Satan's five-alarm atomic butt-burner".   As far as I can tell – that's their loss.   You put a jalapeno on a woman's nacho... she'll look at you like you just put rat poison in her drink. She'll look at you like you're trying to kill her. Calm down, sweetheart... it's just a little flavor.

On the other hand - a real man doesn't even consider food spicy... unless his hind-end is barking for three days afterwards. He doesn't just want his taste buds to go into shock... he wants the enamel melted off his teeth an' his lips fixing to blister. He wants his eye-balls sweating... an' his throat to swell up shut. He wants to eat stuff so hot... he hallucinates!!!   He wants a' waitress to bring the hot wings to the table... wearing a Hazmat suit... with asbestos gloves.

An' then he wants to give her a wink an' go..."You got some hot sauce I can put on these, darlin...?"

Wake up, America. So as far as the guy in England killing himself with his own chili... us real men understand. An' look at the bright side – at least he died before he had to go to the bathroom. I'm Earl Pitts, American. Pitts Off.

Working Out

You know what makes me sick? You know what makes me so mad I just wanna spend the night in a rat infested building... wearing a Green Bay Packers cheese-head?

Yeah – let me ask you a question. Do I look healthier to you? Because the last couple days... I've been going to the gym. I know... I always said no real man had to go to no stupid gym. For a real man work-out... we've got something we call - life! If we wanted to work out with weights... we'd just go to prison.

But see – what happened was this cute young thing in some spandex workout clothes come down to the bowling alley the other night... an' she was passing out free trial one-month gym memberships down at the Stretch an' Squat.   Leastways that's what we call the place...

An' anyway... Joylee... that's the honey in the spandex - she says she's there all the time. An' she gives a lot of attention to new trial members. Fifteen guys in the bar signed up that night. I never figured that many guys were in to physical fitness.

Okay – there's a reason how come rednecks don't join your exercising clubs. **Number one** – we don't look good exercising.   Me an' the Meeker boys started up down there about four night backs... we don't got no Yuppie exercising clothes. We don't got no $150 dollar exercising shoes... or them Richard Simmons exercising headbands. No sir – we were wearing cut-offs ... Harley shirts... an' work boots.

Man, and those people were staring at us like Larry, Darryl an' Darryl just crashed a White House state dinner. I ain't saying we felt a little out of place... but we were a little like the Three Stooges at a MENSA convention. Pretty easy to pick out.

And here's another thing. You know all those people you see in them exercising commercials on the TV? These are *not* the people at the actual exercising gym. There ain't no rock hard bodies with six-pack abs at the exercising club. No – these people look like the rejects on that Biggest Loser show. Apparently turned away - for bein' too fat.

Of course - not everybody there was fat. They also had a healthy supply of' old guys in muscle shirts. It looks a little like a training camp for the hereafter.

But we've been going there anyways. Although - they might kick us out after last night. See – what happened was... Junior Meeker was on the leg press machine. Sucker was pressing 250 pounds... that's pretty impressive. An' me an' Dub Meeker were noodling this thing... and figured if he could press 250 pounds – an' we were to jack up the weight to say... 500 pounds... well, then naturally - Junior would get in shape two times as fast. Makes sense, right? I mean, this free membership is only for a month, you know. We don't have a lot of time.

So when Junior wasn't looking, we threw another 250 pounds on there. Unfortunately - Junior was in the legs-extended position at the time. Now - I don't completely understand the physics of the thing - but Junior actually squirted out of the chair... flew across the gym... an' landed in the middle of a Zumba class.

I don't know if his body got any stronger... but his language did.

Wake up, America. I'll give those exercising people this – we all do feel better working out. Except Junior's been walking funny... an' you don't even want to know what Dub did on the treadmill. I'm Earl Pitts, American. Pitts Off.

Bar Codes on Women

You know what makes me sick? You know what makes me so angry I just wanna join that Internet dating service for redneck girls from the south – E-Hominy.com?

Yeah – me and the boys down at the Duck Inn came up with a' idea last night. It's going to revolutionize dating. In fact, it could change the entire relationship between men and women.

See – what happened was this. We' were setting there, you know… when Runt Wilson's brother, Woodrow walked in there… looking like his dog or his truck just died… or both.

Well, Old Runt… he's wanting to give his brother the business, you know. So he goes, 'Hey, Woody… what about that sweet young thing you walked outta here with last night…?'

Woody goes…'Yeah, after we left the bar… she took me straight to her house." An' we all go, "Yeah buddy… all right!". He goes… "Where I met her mother." An' we're all… "Ohh…" He goes… "an' her six cats…" "Oh'. He goes… "An… her three kids…"

Man – that killed the buzz…

Earl Pitts

Well, Woody pulls up a stool and he goes... "How come you can't find stuff like that out about a woman before you do something you hope you're gonna regret?" And that right there is when the lightning bolt of ingenuity gob-smacked us right upside the head.

Women need barcodes. Yeah – you put one a' those barcodes on their bellies, or their shoulders or somewhere... an then you can scan them before you get too far down the dating path... I mean – let's say you're in a bar... you had a couple a' beers – all you see is hooters, a butt an' hair like Sara Evans. Time to make your move... with the hand held scanner. Yeah - she's been divorced twice... in jail three time for credit card fraud... an' is the sad carrier of her mama's freakishly large giant butt genes...

An' I know barcodes on women would work... because I remember one time, my old lady leaned across the grocery check-out to give the girl a coupon... an ' the machine read her stretch marks... an' rung up a side of beef. So, I know the technology exists.

Wake up, America. But until then... until we get all women tagged with barcodes... an' a national data-base established... buyer beware! I'm Earl Pitts, American. Pitts Off.

Car Names

You know what makes me sick? You know what makes me so angry I just wanna dig up Henry Ford... bring him back to life... an' make him promise he won't die again...?

Because they started screwing up cars right after he died. I'll tell you that. And don't get me wrong. I love cars. I love trucks. I love car dealers. That is not the problem.

The thing I miss the most about the good old days... is car names. Remember when these idiots liked their own products enough... to come up with names for them? It seemed like a harmless enough idea. If you made a car... you called it something. I mean... you had your Duster... and your Mustang... a Charger and a Firebird. Your Nova... and your Taurus... your Camaro. You even had the AMC Gremlin for crying out loud. That thing shouldn't have even been *made.* But they not only made it – *they gave it a name*! I mean...even your crap cars... like your Pinto and your Vega... at least they got names.

I been listening to our new car ads. You know what they got out there now. Your XJ, your GTI, the Q7, A3, A4 and A6... the XA, XB and TC... the 9-2x, 9-3 an' 9-5 sedan. You got the CX-9... the RX-8 and the XC-90. The CTS, the STS and the DTS. Oh... I forgot the G6... the 300... the H3 an' the F-150.

Earl Pitts

That ain't naming a car. That's being lazy. They don't even sound like car names. They sound like bra sizes... or another planet. "Hey, nice pair a' CX-9's you got there..."

What happened... with all those recession cut-backs... did they fire the guys that used to think up the names?

And here's another thing about your vehicles of today. Nobody cares about the engines no more. Remember when you used to buy a truck on how many horses it had under the hood... instead of how many electric doo-dads it had on the dashboard?.

Like last night down at the Duck Inn, Junior Meeker walks in there with a pie-eating grin on his face. He looked like the cat just ate a canary... dipped in mouse blood. And he announced - he just got himself a new truck.

Well – we go running outside to look at it... an' that sucker is a beauty. I mean, he's got that thing tricked out like you would not believe. You know how when you watch those truck commercials on the TV and they say it's $28,000 dollars... an' then they got little words on the TV screen... says $35,000 – as shown. Yeah – well Junior bought himself one... as shown.

But here's what I don't get. He's got a gizmo in that truck... tells him where he's at... at all times. He can't get lost. He says he can put in a address where he wants to go... an' his truck will find the way.

What the hell does a man need that for?   I say it is every red-blooded American man's right... to get lost. Some of the most interesting places I ever been to... I found looking for someplace else.   And number two... a real man doesn't need no computer directions. I believe Lewis and Clark didn't have any GPS system -and they found the Pacific Ocean just fine... thank you very much.

And then he's got another gizmo in there... when he hits a tree... the machine will call an' ambulance.   I mean – isn't one of the big moments in every man's life... the first time he has to crawl back to the road? He says –"Earl – if I ever run off the road... down a gully... flip over an' get pinned in my truck... the emergency people can find me... just like that."

Well – I didn't wanna say nothing... because it already happened to him – twice.   The last time it took us four days to find him...

Wake up, America! Man – we're kind of hoping he skids off the road tonight... so we can see how this thing works.   Call me old fashioned... but the only electronics I need in my truck... is a radio. And maybe a CB. I'm Earl Pitts, American. Pitts off.

Earl Pitts

Man Fantasy Camp

You know what makes me sick? You know what makes me so angry I just wanna go to some fancy-butt, stiff-neck yuppie wedding... an' when the preacher asks if anybody objects... I'd jump up an' yell... "I'm having her baby...!"

I know... It don't make no sense... that's what I like about it.

Let me ask you a question. Have you ever seen those "fantasy camps" they got out there? Like they got a baseball fantasy camp... where you go somewhere for a week an' play baseball? And now they got a NASCAR fantasy camp... where you go somewhere for a week an' learn to drive a stock car... even get to race against a pro...

Well – me an' my buddy Dub Meeker... we got this idea... It's a fantasy camp. Where regular guys, just like you and me can go for a week an' pretend to be the one thing every single one of us wanted to be at one time or the other.

A Real Man. That's right - Fantasy Man Camp. An' we ain't talking about no metro-sexuals... none a' these touchy-feely soccer dads. We're talking about "real" men. We're talking knuckle-draggin', mouth-breathin' real men who can scratch their privates with one hand while they shoot out a snot-wad with the other. We're

Wake Up America!!!

talking about men who think "hygiene"... is what you say when you see your friend, Gene.

I mean... we figured the other night... there must be millions of men out there right now... who have never done nothing manly.   You know – maybe you were brung up by a mama in a broke home. Maybe you was brung up by one a' them whipped "sensitive" Yuppie dads. Whatever the reason -it's probably not your fault. But give us just a week... an' we'll give you the "man" experience.

If you never took a leak balancing off the end of a bass-boat in two-foot waves... you need Man Fantasy Camp. If you've never been so drunk you woke up with a ugly woman... or a farm animal... you need Man Fantasy Camp.   An' if you think a Lap Dance... is the national dance of Lapland... you better call right now!

Wake up, America. I ain't saying we can make men out of y'all in a week's time. But for three-thousand, four-hundred an' ninety-five dollars... not including airfare and meals... we'll see what we can do. I'm Earl Pitts... I'll be manning the phones. Pitts Off.

Peeing in Private

You know what makes me sick? You know what makes me so angry I just wanna drink a case a beer... and hold it. And hold it. And hold it. To find out if my eyeballs really would float...?

I've got a question today... I don't think nobody never asked.   It's this... how come women get to pee in private... an' men go to a wall a' urinals looks like a Amish barn at milking time?

I'm not saying I ain't manly an' can't handle it.   It's just not fair.   I mean... think about this... a woman gets a little stall... set down quiet time all to herself... so what does she do? She takes somebody in there with her.

Now your man... he doesn't need no pee-buddy... he's capable of doing the work by his lonesome. In fact... he prefers to go alone. So he walks in there all by himself... an' lines up with five other guys he ain't never seen before.

I mean — think about this - why do they call them our privates... if they ain't gonna be private?!   And again - I'm not complaining. I'm just wondering.

An' while I'm at it... this is a message just for the men out there... Do you think you could hit the stinking urinal? Lord — don't never invite me to your house. That has got to be one sad bathroom at your home. I mean... I have been in some public restrooms... I needed hip-waders.

An' since we're on the subject - how come they come up with them urinals that flush all by themselves? You know – I always appreciated having something to do with my free hand. You women probably don't know this... but we got these johns now... where they flush by themselves when you finish your business. Problem is... some guys like to hit the flusher before they go. Some men like to hear running water while they go. So you end up doing the Urinal Hokey-Pokey... to get things just right.

Come to think of it... maybe that's when the floor gets wet. When you turn yourself around... That's what it's all about...

Wake up, America. Women like to complain they make less money than men... they don't run enough companies... there isn't no woman president. Yeah – but you get to take a leak in private. That makes us even. I'm Earl Pitts, American. Pitts Off.

Earl Pitts

Fishing Cheats

You know what makes me sick? You know what makes me so mad I just wanna lick the slime off a sick carp?

I think I just figured out the definition of "redneck". That's doing the same stupid stuff over and over... expecting things to come out different.

Like you keep getting' in fights with your old lady... convinced sooner or later God's gonna let you win one. Like that's gonna ever happen.

Like every time you walk into a bar... you hope you don't get drunk an' do something stupid. Like that's ever gonna *NOT* happen...

Then I saw where two good old redneck boys in Kentucky done the exact same thing me an' Dub Meeker tried ten years ago. An' just like us – they got caught. I could have told them it was gonna happen.

See – what happened was this. There was a fishing tournament over there ... these old boys figured out a way to win first prize... which happened to be a brand new thirty-thousand dollar bass boat.

So what they done was... they caught some big old fish before the tournament... an' put them in wire cages under water. Once the fishing started, those boys took off right to the cages... pulled out prize winners - and

Wake Up America!!!

got caught.

I am not proud of this... but a ways back... me and the Meeker boys tried that. Except we didn't catch big fish. We caught little fish an' kept them in my bathtub for nine months. Then we fed them and fattened them up. It was a good plan.

I'll tell you how much thinking we put in this. We even kept the fish blindfolded... so they could not identify us. So we weren't total idiots.

And we would have gotten away with it too. Except we slipped up. When we were in the bathroom feeding the fish... we used our real names. Dumb, dumb, dumb...

Wake up, America. As God is my witness... I did not know fish had ears. Anyways... if you're thinking about rigging a bass tournament... been there... don't do that. I'm Earl Pitts, American. Pitts Off.

Earl Pitts

Survivor Man

You know what makes me sick? You know what makes me so angry I just wanna eat me a box of dry Alky-Seltzer tablets… drink a Mountain Dew… and then jump on a pogo stick?

We were having an argument at the Duck Inn last night… which one of us had the best chances of surviving in the wild. You've seen those survivor shows they got on the TV now, right? Yeah, they take one of these certified nut-ball idiots… they blindfold him… take him out in the middle of God knows where… an' leave him. And then he's got to survive for seven days with just a Swiss Army knife an' a poncho. Well – that an' enough video gear to broadcast the Olympics… but you get the idea.

Yeah – he survives by his training and his wits. You know what they call that, don'tcha? That's the "Redneck Disneyland" right there.

I mean, there is not a man alive on this earth any "real" man at least - that doesn't dream of living off the land. That's your redneck Fantasyland. Staring down death. Surviving against overwhelming odds. Wrestling snakes an' alligators. I'm getting' chicken-skin just thinking about it.

Number one… I know I could do it. Because I'm too ornery to die. I mean, you drop me in a swamp for

Wake Up America!!!

seven days... I wouldn't be building no lame lean-to an' no dinky raft. Hell... inside a' week I'd have me a hand-made double-wide an' a carved-out bass boat. Lord, I'd be cutting down more trees than Georgia-Pacific. Inside a' three days... I'd be trading beaver pelts with the Indians for a squaw. The question ain't could I survive. The question would be... *could the wilderness survive...* with me in it? I doubt it.

Dub Meeker goes... he could survive out in the wilderness, too. I go, "Dub... you can't take a leak in the woods... cause you think the animals are watching...." Dub says... "He'd hold it..."   He says he could live by his wits for a week...

I go... Well... if you were living by your wits... you'd at least make it a half-week.

Wake up, America. I mean, I hate to bust the boy's bubble... but Dub Meeker ain't cut out for no surviving... Every winter we go hunting... he thinks the Deliverance boys are gonna get him. You ain't exactly Jeremiah Meeker, old buddy. I'm Earl Pitts, American. Pitts Off.

Earl Pitts

CHAPTER TWO
FAMILY LIFE

A Romantic Night

You know what makes me sick? You know what makes me so mad I just wanna throw my old lady down on a bed covered with roses... with the thorns still attached??

Yeah – I thought I'd do something nice for my wife last night. I says, "Pearl... your birthday is coming up, girl – what do you want?" An' she goes, "Earl... know what I want more than anything in the whole world? I want a nice romantic night out with my husband."

And I go, "Okay – what would be number two...?"

Yeah – that'll teach me. Never ask your old lady what she wants – ever. Just get her that Walmart gift card... an' get out of the way.

Anyway – she goes on and on about how the romance has gone out of our marriage. She says I never make her feel like she did when we were dating anymore.

Well – I got a theory about that. Let's say you were a cheetah... an' it was your job to chase down an kill a gazelle. So you chase that gazelle... 60-miles a hour... twisting and turnin' up a storm. You're jumping bushes... kicking up dust. An' then you finally catch that old gazelle. Why on earth would you let it get back up an' start chasing it again...

And for those of you a little slow on the up-take... the

Earl Pitts

gazelle is your old lady. Once you catch her - the chasing part should be over. I don't know – maybe I'm watching too much Animal Planet.

Anyway... she says I ain't romantic any more. I'll show her romantic. I'm gonna take a shower. I'm gonna shave... an' I'm gonna take her to the Applebee's. That's right. Yeah – George Clooney can eat my shorts.

And then... bowling. An' not just any bowling neither... moonlight bowling... with the disco ball and the lights.

Then we'll stop on the way home behind the power plant... an' make out in the truck. If she's still small enough to do that...

Wake up, America! Then when we get home... maybe a bath together in the dark. We don't have no candles... but I do have a couple of road flares. That ought to be enough romance for another decade. I'm Earl Pitts, American. Pitts Off!!!

Painting

You know what makes me sick? You know what makes me so mad I just wanna practice for the rodeo... by riding that paint shaker at the hardware store??

Yeah – the other day my old lady says she wants to paint the dining room. Now – I don't mind painting... it's almost like real construction. Except for any tool made out of hair... is a pretty wimpy tool. But here is something I found out very interesting - women love to paint.

But women an' men paint different. Like a woman will go to the hardware store and look at those 512 different shades of green paint strips for four hours. A man will go in there... and see if anybody returned a' unused can. He don't even care what the color is... if it's cheap.

An' then your women will take the top five green paint strips over to the curtain aisle... an' hold them up against the closest thing they got to your curtains. Your man -would already be halfway home.

Your woman will take out a calculator and figure the square footage of the room, multiplied by two coats... divided by the estimated coverage of the gallon – to make a pinpoint purchase. Your man... is getting two cans. An' if that means the closets don't get painted again... so be it.

Earl Pitts

An' then your women are gonna buy every dang painting doo-dad they sell. Three different size rollers... two different brushes... edgers... masking tape... drop cloth ... sponges... pans... knives... Your man... would already have the furniture pulled away from the wall.

An' then your women will get into a deeply philosophical discussion with the paint guy about the benefits of eggshell, satin, flat... or semi-gloss. Your man – would already be on the second coat.

Wake up America!! Anyways good news - we got this brand new bright and shiny dining room. Bad news... my old lady's still serving the same ol' crap food in there. Turns out – the color was not the problem. I'm Earl Pitts, American. Pitts Off.

Pearl's Mad

You know what makes me sick? You know what makes me so mad I just wanna do a naked cannon-ball dive into a pricker patch?

Yeah… I just had me a lost weekend. An' I wasn't even drunk. I mean… don't get me wrong… I wanted to be drunk. This was definitely a drinking weekend. And I didn't, and I wasn't. What I was - was in a state of turmoil.

See, what happened was… Friday night I was working down at The Duck Inn an' my good old buddy, Dub Meeker comes in there like he just seen ghost.

He goes… "Earl… son - you are in some deep, deep trouble." Only he didn't say "trouble"… I'm cleaning it up to the PG level. He goes on to tell me his old lady was talking to my old lady… An' my old lady was madder than a Rottweiler with a toothache. I mean, she told his old lady… she wasn't gonna take it no more. Things were going to change! And she meant 'big time'.

In other words… Dub Meeker knows how to ruin a Friday night.

I mean, we spent two hours… trying to figure out what I done wrong. He goes… "Did she tell you to do something… an' you didn't do it?" I'm thinking… "Every day!!" He goes… "Was she maybe talking to you and you were ignoring her?" And I'm thinking ... "Every day!!!"

So I get home Friday night... and she ain't talking to me. I get up Saturday morning, right... and I cleaned up the whole yard. I put all the cinder blocks back next to the house... cleaned up the ditch. She still wasn't talking. So I changed the oil in her car... the oil I promised I'd change in November. I did it. Uh uh... an' she still wasn't talking.

So I cleaned out the garage... replaced the belt on the dryer... fixed the handle on the toilet. I even took EJ to ball practice... and that woman was *still* looking sour. I mean, she had a face on her... like she had an ingrown toenail... on a hemorrhoid.

Finally... I got a little angry myself. That's usually not like me. But I had enough. I go... 'Pearl... I don't know what I did to you. I don't know what I said to you... But there is nothing I could ever say or do to deserve you being this mad...

She goes...'"You??? I'm mad at your daughter..."

Crap.

Wake up, America. That's really not fair. Women should have a sign on their foreheads... so you can tell who they're mad at. I mean I hope she doesn't get mad at me next weekend... everything's fixed. I'm Earl Pitts, American. Pitts Off.

Island Life

You know what makes me sick? You know what makes me so mad I just wanna get on that there Travel Channel... so I can schedule 24-straight hours of programs... about Mudd Lake? Hey - you can only take so much Vegas.

Yeah – you know what my old lady told me last night? Let me tell you – this woman is a piece a' work. She says... get this... she wants to run away... an' live on a island the rest of her life.

Yeah – I got a' island for you, Pearl. Alcatraz!!! Devil's Island! The Island of ' No Return! Take your pick – you nitwit!

See – she watches all those travel shows on the TV... an' she gets hepped up 'bout that island life. Setting there in the ocean... drinking those froo-froo sissy drinks with them little umbrellas.

Then she watches them Kenny Chesney video and that sawed- off little runt is always singing on some island. Then she watches Wheel of Fortune... an' they're all the times giving away trips to Hawaii. So my old lady has got an island bug up her butt... and I know she didn't get this crap for me.

So let me set you straight, Pearl. We ain't gonna be living on no god-forsook, malaria-infested topical island.

45

Earl Pitts

An' I'll tell you how come.   **Reason number one**... I don't wanna see my old lady wearing one of those coconut bras.   'Cause if you've seen those island shows... all the women on those islands wear coconut bras.   Not only does that look like it hurts... an' might be slightly unsanitary... it's also gotta confuse the hell out of the monkeys.

Number two... I am too old to learn to dance with fire. That's right.   That's another thing you see on all those traveling shows.   All island people love to dance with sticks on fire.   Lord, my hair is so greasy... one bad move... an' I'd go up like a torch.   I can't risk something like that...

Then most of your tropical islands are inhabited by one of two different types of native.   Your head-hunters... and your cannibals.   So when I say "pick your poison"... in most cases, they don't give you a choice.   You go with the house brand.

And then my old lady goes... "You can fish for giant marlins, Earl"

So - we have not totally ruled it out... neither.

Wake up, America!   I mean, I would like to catch a fish bigger than me before I die.

And if that means Pearl dancing in a grass skirt... hey, she's the one risking butt – chiggers... not me.   I'm Earl Pitts, American. Pitts Off.

Decorator Flags

You know what makes me sick? You know what makes me so mad I just wanna play duck, duck, goose - with actual waterfowl?

Yeah — the other day my old lady said she wanted me to put a couple more flag poles on our front porch. Now you know me... I love old glory, so if my old lady doesn't think our two flags is enough and we need two more... well, by golly — I'm all for it. And to tell you the truth... I was kind of proud of the old girl. For a little bit, anyway...

Up until two hours later... when I got those flag brackets on the porch... an' she came out of the house with the flags. The first one was a flag of a frog setting on a inner tube wearing sunglasses an' drinking a margarita through a crazy-straw.

Now I don't know what country has that flag... but it sure as hell ain't America! I go, "What in the world, woman... that ain't no stars an' stripes...!" She goes, "Earl..that's our summer flag... it's cute."

People, let me explain somethin' to you. Flags aren't supposed to be cute. Flags are there for one reason... to fill you with pride... an' scare the crap out or your enemy. Somehow I don't think a frog drinking a margarita is gonna do the job.

Earl Pitts

The only flag you need to fly... is the American flag. And that ain't got no frogs on it. A flag is supposed to have red on it... for blood. White on it... for virginity... an' blue on it... ahhh.....to remind us how cold it got at Valley Forge.

Okay... and you can fly a #3 flag... in honor of the memory of Dale Senior. That's it.

Okay... an' maybe a POW/MIA flag... but that's it. That's really it.

Then my old lady pulls out her second flag... you thought the drunken frog was embarrassing... this one had a pink flamingo in a hula skirt... wearing sunglasses...

Lord, the VFW is gonna firebomb our house!

Wake up, America. When our brave boys raised that flag on Iwo Jima... I don't remember no flamingo in a hula skirt on it. If you're gonna fly a flag – fly the only one that counts. Old Glory. I'm Earl Pitts, American. Pitts Off.

Getting Sick

You know what makes me sick? You know what makes me so angry I just wanna chug a quart a' Nyquil... and then operate heavy machinery? ...Just for the hell of it!

Yeah – I been getting' me a little bit a' the head-snots here lately. It's that time of year, you know.   I've got stuff coming' out of my nose... that could star in its own horror movie.

Anyways... I heard this story the other day. They did some research over there in England - and they found when a husband or a wife gets sick... the man treats the sick woman... a lot better than the woman treats the sick man. Yeah – these experts said a man will baby his old lady if she gets sick. He'll cook for her... do her cleaning.   He will wait on her hand and foot.

On the other hand, a woman will feel sorry for the sick man... a' average of five minutes!!!

Man – you don't have to go to England to find that out. Just come over to the Pitts house.

I swear to you... here's the deal. I started getting' this snot thing 'bout two days ago.   You know the first thing my old lady did? She was figuring out what I must of done wrong to catch a cold. It was like a Congressional subcommittee hearing. She wasn't interested in solving the problem. She just wanted to affix the blame. "I told you not to go outside without a coat on, Earl!" "I told you not to go outside with your hair wet, Earl!" "I told you to wear socks, Earl!" Yap, yap, yap, yap!!!

You know when your nose starts to running... and your ears start to plugging up...and your head starts to pounding... yeah that is about the most perfect time to take a load of crap from someone who professes to be a loved one.

An' then... *then* she accuses you of *faking* two quarts a' mucus pouring out your head cavities every day... so you don't gotta do stuff with her. "Oh," she says... "I guess Earl's got a head-cold... so he can't help with the Christmas shopping... *again*!!!"

Yeah - you get a little sick... you're hoping your old lady will turn into Florence Nightingale. More than likely - she'll turn into that chick in the movie, Misery... the one with the sledgehammer.

Oh – and by the way... no matter what kind of medicine you buy... it's not gonna work as good as what she would of bought. Because – apparently she's a professional healer... an' you're a idiot!!!

Wake up, America! Let's face facts men – we're all gonna get sick. Some of us are gonna catch the flu. But *all* of us are gonna catch some grief. It's the season.

Grocery Cart Shame

You know what makes me sick? You know what makes me so mad I just wanna go to the circus an' slap a clown? Who am I kidding - I'd even like to do that when I'm happy.

Anyways – they got a story out there… says tough times in the economy can make you fat. Yeah – so my old lady got something else to blame.

See - what it is… they say when people don't have much money… they buy up all that cheap fattening foods… like macaroni an' cheese in the box. And they buy up that stuff on the fast food dollar menu.

Now – maybe I'm wrong… but it seems to me we were getting' fat during the good times, too. Hell – I've been gaining weight since the day I was born. I mean – look at me – I don't think I'm ever gonna get back to 7-pounds, 8-ounces.

But anyway – this story got me to thinking. My old lady introduced me to something I never heard of before. I call it – "grocery cart shame." Yeah – grocery cart shame. That's when you run into somebody you know at the grocery store… an' your cart is loaded up with junk food.

We were down at the store the other day… mindin' our own business… buying what we buy. Yeah - and then

Earl Pitts

my old lady runs into one of her friends from church. Well – she went into a full-blown tizzy... trying to hide down the aisles. Then we heard, "Pearl, Pearl..."

This old gal come wheeling up to us... and my ol' lady is just shaking her head. It looks like the woman had a garden in her grocery cart. She got all sorts a' vegetables... fruits... bottled water. And while she's talking - she's also sizing up our cart. We've got hot dogs... donuts... Coco Pebbles... beer... brownies... Rice-a-Roni... spaghetti... bacon... an' ice cream.

When this woman takes off... my old lady looks at our shopping cart and she looks at me an goes..."Earl, I hope she didn't think we were gonna eat all this crap..." And I go, "No, Pearl... she obviously thought we were just moving it back and forth between different aisles..."

Wake up, America. So we zipped over to the produce aisle... an' grabbed some lettuce an' oranges... to hide the good stuff. 'Cause you never know who you're gonna run into. I'm Earl Pitts, American. Pitts Off.

Gas

You know what makes me sick? You know what makes me so mad I just wanna chew on tinfoil?

Y'all are gonna find this hard to believe... but sometimes I run outta stuff to talk about. So last night I'm setting in the kitchen with a pad a' paper, and I couldn't come up with anything.

So my old lady goes... "You know what makes *me* sick, Earl? Why don't you talk about how gassy you are? Why don't you talk about the suffering of your wife with you breaking wind 24/7! Why don't you talk about how rude that is... and how it totally ignores the comfort of your family!"

In case you didn't t figure it out... I had just ripped one. Excuse me. Okay – let's talk about the passing of gas. Your trouser sneeze... a boxer burp. Or as I like to call it – butt yodeling.

First of all... let's state a scientific fact. Women got gas too. We just don't know what they do with most of it. The only thing I can figure... home all day – peeling the wallpaper off the dining room walls.

An' even when you're around them when they let one go... girl gas don't sound like man gas. I don't know... they sound like New Year's noisemakers to me. The only male that would make a noise like that... would be

Earl Pitts

a male chipmunk.

I guess that's how come they feel superior... and can complain about us men. Well – I've got news for you ladies. If that's the biggest complaint you got about your old man... your life is pretty sweet. Even though I know it doesn't smell like it.

Yeah - the fact is... I got gas. Big deal! I always had gas... and after twenty-some odd years... you'd think she'd be used to it. It's not all that different from living near a paper plant.   Best you can hope for... is most days the breeze is blowing the other way.

My old lady says... "Earl... you could at least be considerate and hold it in when you're around people." Yeah – she don't understand a man's body – like she don't understand business. You can't have manufacturing... without distribution.

Wake up, America! That being said... it was a stupid commentary idea, Pearl.   And I am not gonna waste this reader's time talking about what sounds like *your* problem. Whoa – excuse me. I'm Earl Pitts, American. Pitts Off.

CHAPTER THREE
THE AMERICAN LIFE

Earl Pitts

Remember "When" Guys

You know what makes me sick? You know what makes me so mad I just wanna get me a part time job at old folks homes... as an enema tester?

Yeah – I have witnessed a sad passage a' time. A defining moment in every man's life. And it stinks.

See what happened was this – me and the Meeker boys was down at the Duck Inn last night... and Junior Meeker had to run across the road to get a pack a smokes. Well, he comes back in there shaking his head... an' he goes... "I remember when you could buy cigarettes for four dollars a pack!" And Dub laughs... an' he goes... "I remember when you could buy'em for $3.75... *out of a machine!!*"

And I says... "Boys - you heard what just happened there?" An' Dub goes, "Yeah – they're ripping us off on tobacco." An' I go, "No – we just became, *I remember when* guys."

Nobody likes an "I remember when guy". His main purpose in life is to remind people how much better it used to be than it is now.

He remembers when things were cheaper... men were tougher... America was greater... cars were faster... an' every woman was more voluptuous. He remembers when people were poorer... but happier. And he remembers when it snowed more... the summers were hotter... fall leaves were prettier... an' everybody was friendlier.

In other words... it's mostly BS... but the mind can play tricks on you when you get older. An' when you're under the age of say... 40... an' you run into a "I remember when guy"... you just kind of ignore him. Chalk him up as a crazed old coot stuck in the land of "Usedtabe"... where everything "usedtabe" better.

And then one day... I don't know what happens... it might be like a biological clock thing or something... you wake up... an' you're that guy. And here's the weird part – I remember when... I wasn't.   How's that for ironic?

Wake up, America! Then, once we get a little older... we can add the word "back". We'll be, I remember "back" when guys. I'd say there's no looking back when we got to that point... but the fact is - there's *only* looking back when we get to that point. I'm Earl Pitts, American. Pitts Off.

Earl Pitts

Not a People Person

You know what makes me sick? You know what makes me so angry I just wanna give Richard Simmons a wedgie?   Because I know − if there is one person on earth who'd enjoy that... it would probably be him.

You know who I hate?   An' before you start listing everybody and their lame-butt brother... hang on − I got a new one. I hate, people-people.

You know what I'm talking 'bout, right? Like a people person... some yokel that loves bein' around people. A real "life of the party."   Well − more than that one people person... is people-people. I could be totally off on that... but just follow along.

Yeah − people tell me all the time when they hear I'm a suds jockey... they go − "Earl, you must be a people person."   Yeah − I'm a people person − kinda like, Jack the Ripper was a people person. I mean − he was out on the town almost every night. And the women said the guy was a scream.

Actually − this might come as a shock to you... but I generally do not like people.   I do not like rich people. I do not like poor people. I don't like liberals... enviroweenies... yuppies... soccer fans... pinkos... dopesmokin' tree-huggers...

I do not like people what say Ant... instead a' 'aunt'...

Wake Up America!!!

I do not like people who eat "organic"... I don't like lawyers... dentists... or those dim-wit, knuckle-dragging kids with their pants down around their ying-yangs. I don't like people that take their coffee any way but with milk an' sugar.

I do not like people that tell me I got to get out there and exercise more.

Fact is... if I found somebody that thought just like me. Believed just like me. Had the same 'pinions just like me. Felt the same way about everything just like me. I probably wouldn't like him. And I'm pretty sure he'd feel the same way.

Wake up, America. So don't come in the Duck Inn thinking I'm gonna be your best friend. Shut up... drink up... an' leave. And forgive me if that sounds a little stand-offish. I'm Earl Pitts, American. Pitts Off.

Earl Pitts

A Proud American

You know what makes me sick? You know what makes me so mad I just wanna lock myself in a used Port-a-Let... until I'm overtaken by the fumes?

Now – I know there are some god-fearing, red-blooded, right-thinking Americans out there that have their panties a little twisted right now. Y'all are worried the liberal pinko commies have took over in this country.

You think before you know it... we'll be redistributing wealth... standing in line for free food... and taking God out of our pledges and our oaths.

Hey - as crazy as all that sounds... if anything even remotely close to that happened - guess what?
All you have to do – is do what I'm gonna do. I refuse to participate. If those nanny-state, tree-huggin' liberal twits wanna take over this country... an' ruin it. They are not gonna have Earl Pitts helping them. I promise that.

Number one – I am not marrying another man. I don't care how trendy it is. I'm gonna keep having sex with women. Call me a throw-back. I don't care.

Number two – I am gonna continue to eat meat. And I mean lots of meat. Lots and lots of meat. I mean - I'm gonna sweat sausage grease. And enjoy every dang minute of it.

Number three - I am not driving no dinky little hy-breed clown car. When somebody asks me how come I'm still driving an eight-cylinder truck... I'm gonna say... 'cause they don't make a ten-cylinder. An' then... I'm gonna peal out.

Number four - y'all come for my guns. You better bring *your* guns. An' you better know how to use them.

Number five - I will not turn my back on the Almighty. I will not take God out of the pledge... I will not take God out of Christmas. You might be able to separate church and state... but you won't be separating church from Earl Pitts.

And I know God's got my back on that one.

Wake up, America. You can whine an' fuss like a baby with a dirty diaper cause the liberals took over. Or you can stand your ground an' fight. As one great American once said... Let's Roll!! I'm Earl Pitts, American. Pitts Off.

Buying a Phone

You know what makes me sick? You know what makes me so mad I just wanna arm-wrestle... a Silver-Back Gorilla?

I think y'all know by now... I have decided not to participate in the technology revolution. That's right – I'm goin' all Unabomber on the rest of the world.

Yeah – to me... I like the old fashioned phones. And by that - I mean the ones stuck to the wall in the kitchen. with a gnarled cord strung half-ways to Kingdom come. Hell, they lost me when they got rid of the dial. I don't need no i-Phone... p-Phone... g-Phone or d-Phone.

Course, you know my old lady... she's keeping up with all this stuff. Or pretends she is, anyways, and she told me last night... she said, "Earl... we're gonna go and get you a new phone." So we went over last night to that fancy whizz-bang phone store. I think it was called "Geek Heaven". Or at least that what I thought the sign said.

Yeah - it was like walking onto the bridge of the StarShip Enterprise... I know Captain Kirk said hello to me. This is where some pencil-necked dweebs go out of their way to make you feel inferior. I mean – you don't even walk up to the counter an' ask for help, no more. You log onto their computer... an' put your name in line. All the while - the dork is standing right there behind the

Wake Up America!!!

counter... but he can't see you... *until you put your stinking name in the dang computer!!!*

Well – I was about to put my fist in his computer - but I think Captain Kirk finally looked up and must have felt sorry for us mere mortals. He asked what we needed... an' my old lady says "my husband needs a new phone."

He looks at me and he goes... "What do you want to do with your phone?" An' I go... "Hmmmmm... Talk to people, Sherlock!!!" Well he looks at my old lady... an' they both roll their eyes. That's wonderful... you're getting' tag-teamed and belittled by your old lady an' the captain of the High School AV Squad.

He says... "Are you gonna text." I go, "No."   He goes, "Are you gonna take pictures?" I go, "No."   He goes, "Are you gonna access the Internet or download apps?" I go, "No."   He goes... "Are you gonna tweet?" I go, "No, I'm gonna Twalk. To my fwiends!!!"

Wake up, America!   Yeah – I think I stumped him. Apparently in today's America... I am the missing link. But I did get a phone. I just don't know how to work it yet. I'm Earl Pitts, American. Pitts Off.

The Hitchhiker

You know what makes me sick? You know what makes me so mad I just wanna pick up a scary hitchhiker in the middle of the night... with a wild look in his eyes... an' a hook...???

People ask me sometimes... "Earl, is it ever okay to pick up a hitch-hiker?"

Well - you can never be too careful. There are a lot of crazies out there these days. But at the same time... there's a lot a' totally innocent people need a lift. There's a fine line out there between being a good neighbor... an' being in a shallow grave somewhere off Highway 19. So this is a tricky question.

First of all - let me just say... the quality of your hitchhiker has gone to hell the past few years. I mean... I remember when your hitchhikers were your hobos... or your dope-smokin' hippies... maybe some jacked up high school kids... I mean ... they all put some pride into it.

Today... it's like a derelict convention out there on the side of the road. And they don't proudly stick that thumb out like a real hitchhiker neither... giving you the old thumb wave... pumping that sucker for all it's worth... that arm stuck out like they were serious.

Wake Up America!!!

No... today... it looks like their arm is broken... just dangling there... with some pathetic thumb half out.

They don't even have the gumption to degrade themselves with any kind of energy. Hell - I don't know why I should take the energy to stop... when you can't even get up the energy to thumb right.

An' that bein' said... I did pick up a hitchhiker last night. An' that's where I come to the safety part. I know... I know... picking up a hitchhiker might be dangerous. But I've got a way to play it safe. See - I only pick up people who don't look as scary as me. I want some loser getting in my truck already more scared of me than I am of him. That way – if things get out of hand in the truck... I naturally got the upper hand.

Anyhow... this old boy climbs in the truck... he got a duffle bag with him... says he's getting out of town. Then he just shuts up... for like ten miles. He's kind of looking at me... I'm kind of looking at him.

Finally I go... "Hey, buddy... you wouldn't be some kind of whacked-out, evil-doin' serial killer would you?" He goes "No..."

An' I go... "Good... cause how weird a coincidence would that be....?"

Wake up, America. I don't mind picking you people up... I just wish you'd let me slow down before you jumped out. Last I seen him... he was cartwheeling down a highway embankment. Didn't even say thank you. I'm Earl Pitts, American. Pitts Off.

Born in the USA

You know what makes me sick? You know what makes me so angry I just wanna kick a grizzly bear... in the groin?

I am so sick and tired of these mouth-breathing idiots out there whining about America. "We lost our way, we're going in the wrong direction, the economy stinks."

Well – let me tell you thumb-sucking cry-babies something. An' listen up good, ya' pant-loads.

The greatest thing that ever happened to you – you had nothing to do with. You were born in America. The doctor slapped your butt an' you started screaming... in America. You took your first breath... in America. Your mama put you to her breast... in America.

Hell – you could have been born in France. Or Russia. Or some god-forsook worthless jerk-burger, back-water hell-hole third world country. But no – you were born in America. It's like you hit the lottery... an' you didn't even buy a ticket!

So just remember – if y'all wanna whine about America... there's about 5.7-billion people that would gladly change places with you.

And I know... some of you people like to get your panties all wadded up over politics. "This guy can make us great again, this party can save the country." Can we finally all agree... those back-slapping weasels are never gonna be what's best about America.

Because you gotta understand something, people. Presidents and Senators, and faceless thumb-up- their-butt bureaucrats don't make America great. *Americans* make America great.

It's the truck drivers... and the construction workers... and the teachers and the mechanics that make this country great. It's the farmers and the Army men. The guys that put in a hard eight at the plant every day without fail. So if you're setting there on your big fat butt... waiting for Washington to change things... you're dumber than you look. That bus ain't coming.

Get out there... and start working. Shut up – suck it up... an' get moving

If you want America to be great again... how about starting by being a great American.

Wake up, America! Sorry I had to kick you in the teeth like that. But y'all need some sense slapped into you. When you were born in America – you got a 90- yard head-start in a 100-yard race. So shut up – an' keep running. I'm Earl Pitts American. Pitts Off!

Stupid Things People Say

You know what makes me sick? You know what makes me so mad I just wanna goose a moose?

Here's what's bugging me today... the stupid things people say to try to make you feel better. You know – you're feeling puny... something bad happened... and some nitwit wants to feel your pain... by saying something really ,*really* stupid.

Like when you go to the funeral home... hug the widow and look at the dead guy. And you go, "You know... Bill looks so peaceful..." And the widow is thinking, "Yeah - you should have seen him the last five minutes of his life when he was trying to cough up that turkey bone".

I'll give you another example. I saw this story said Bill Gates was worth $50 billion dollars. Yeah – some four-eyed, Poindexter, computer nerd is the richest guy in the world. I was moanin' about it – you know... and you know what my old lady said to me? She goes... Don't worry, Earl... Bill Gates puts his pants on one leg at a time... just like you."

What!?!?! Number one... how in the hell is that supposed to make me feel any better. And number two... now I've got a picture in my head of Bill Gates with no pants on!!

So she goes... "What difference does it make if you have

Earl Pitts

all the money in the world? You can't take it with you".

Pearl – I don't wanna take it with me. I wanna spend it now!! I mean – think about that... is that supposed to make me feel better about not having money... or better about dying? All it did for me – was make me madder than a Chihuahua doing the butt scoots across sandpaper.

Here's another good one... remember back when OJ was found not guilty. Yeah – I took that pretty hard. But you know what my old lady said to me? She said, "Don't worry, Earl ... someday he's gonna have to answer to God" Why couldn't he have to answer to God right away... I don't know – a lightning bolt... earth opens up an' swallows him whole. Something like that.

I've got a list in my head of maybe a half dozen people my old lady says... will have to answer to God. I don't mind God passing the final judgment... I'd just like to be in the courtroom.

Wake up America! Then one day you're setting there... you lost your job, your truck broke down... an' your dog died. Somebody will come up – slap you on the back an' go... It could be worse'. Oh great – jinx!!! I'm Earl Pitts, American Pitts Off.

Raising Monkeys

You know what makes me sick? You know what makes me so angry I just wanna have a banana-eating contest with an orangutan... and win?

I think most of y'all will agree... Earl Pitts and monkeys go way back. I mean – I love my monkeys. I like monkeys in the news. I like monkeys when they got TV shows. Sometimes I like to go to a zoo... just to watch monkeys.

I have always been a big fan of monkeys. In fact – if there was a magazine called *Better Homes and Monkeys*... I would subscribe... twice.

But this story takes the cake. Apparently there are people out there... more monkey crazy than even me. They did this story on the news... I don't know if y'all seen this or not... but some people are so lonely after their kids grow up and leave home... they are adopting monkeys to raise as children.   There's even a name for this... they call them "mon-kids".

Like I said – I love monkeys. But not enough to raise one as my own. Hell – I can't get rid of the two monkeys I got in the house right now.

I mean – how in the world do you raise up a monkey like it was your own kid? Like if I was to take my new son to the barber for his first haircut. Where do they start? That sucker's got a lotta hair!

Then you've got those parent-teacher conferences. "Mr. an' Mrs. Pitts... your son is very disruptive in the class. He don't listen in class... an' throws poop on the other students..." God – that would be embarrassin'.

"I don't know, teacher... he didn't get that at home. Honest!"

Then he's gonna want to get his license when he turns 16. Do y'all know how much insurance would cost for a monkey driver? Honestly - I don't know neither – but I'm guessing it's a lot! Course then he's gonna want to join the high school band. Yeah – probably playing the cymbals...

Wake up, America. I want a monkey – I just don't want to be his daddy. I don't wanna raise him... I just wanna tie him to a stake in the backyard and invite my buddies to come over and watch him do funny stuff. If he thought he was my kid - that would be awkward. I'm Earl Pitts, American. Pitts off.

Illegal Aliens

You know what makes me sick? You know what makes me so mad I just wanna eat a bowl of chili... made with Mexican jumping beans...?? So my belly can burn... an' dance at the same time.

I think I'm on to something here. I gave this careful thought... and I told my buddies down at the Duck Inn last night... I said - I have decided to renounce my United States citizenship.

And Dub Meeker goes, "Don't be stupid, Earl. For all our problems - this is still the best country on earth." He says... "There ain't no country anywhere that is gonna be any better than America."

I says, 'I totally agree with you, Dub... but I didn't say I was moving nowhere... I just ain't gonna be an American"... " I'm gonna be a illegal alien."

Now follow me on this. Let's say, for example, Johnny Law pulls me over some night. What's the first thing he's gonna do? He's gonna ask me for some ID. Now - if I refuse... he's gonna yank me out of the truck - taser my sorry butt... get me on the ground in handcuffs.. an' throw me in a cell with some low-life, riff-raff.

If I was a illegal alien and refused... he'd probably have to apologize... and then have to go through six weeks of

Earl Pitts

sensitivity and profilin' trainin'.

Runt Wilson says... "Yeah - but how often do you get pulled over?" An' I go – "Fair enough - let's talk about yer' healthcare. That Obamacare thing got my insurance premiums shooting through the roof like a horrible hot-water tank accident. Then I got to pay the co-pays... schedule a doctor appointment four months down the line when what I got will have already be disappeared ... or have killed me. That is - *if* I'm an American. If I was an illegal alien... I could go to the emergency room... get same day service... an' not have to pay a dime. An' they legally can't turn me away."

An' I go... "And then let's talk your higher education. Let's say my little boy, Earl Junior wanted to go to college. In some states - children of illegal aliens get preferential treatment getting into college. My little boy is gonna need that preferential stuff - 'cause he's dumber than a tub sponge. An' then - because he'd be the child of a illegal alien... he gets in-state tuition even if I send him out of state. He's stupid - I'm poor - it's like the system is built for us".

Wake up, American. Yeah - it kind of makes you scratch your head, don't it. When you realize the American dream these days... is not being American. We are seriously messed up. I'm Earl Pitts, American. Pitts Off.

CHAPTER FOUR
THE DUCK INN

Earl Pitts

A Life of Disrepute

You know what makes me sick? You know what makes me so mad I just wanna strangle a mule and drag his pack up a mountain?

Man... I had a weird one the other night. Some strange dude I never seen before comes in the bar. He's kind a sad sacking it, you know... drowning himself in longnecks an' keeping to himself. Never a good sign...

So I finally go, "What's up, buddy... you're looking like you got your butt whooped pretty good."

Well - he looks up at me and he goes... "You don't know the half of it." He says his old lady caught him cheating. I go, "Oh man... that's tough." And he goes... "No it gets worse." People in his office caught him embezzling. And I go, "You're right –that is worse." And he goes, "No... then it gets *really* bad." He says he slipped into a life a' drugs an' alcohol... a life of disrepute. He says he lied and cheated... he used his friends... he burned all his bridges and spiraled down to the lowest point in his life".

I go... "Man, that is a bad story." And he goes... "No, then it gets worse." He says he started dabbling in the witchcraft... and made an unholy alliance with the devil. He says Satan himself looked at his life an' said... "I could use you..." He said his own children disowned him... his dog wouldn't even let him pet him.

Wake Up America!!!

He says he became selfish, an desperate... an' paranoid. He even thought about ending it a couple times... but he found he was also a coward.

An' he takes a big old swig from his bottle... slams it on the bar an' goes, "I need another, bartender."

I kinda sniffed a little an' wiped my eyes with the bar towel... I mean, I was moved. I have never seen one man in that much pain. And I go..."What are you gonna do now, buddy?"

He looks at me an' goes... "It depends if I'm re-elected or not."

This would be a good place for a rim shot... if I had a drum.

Wake up, America! Obviously I'm voting for the guy. That's the kind of people we need in Washington. Mostly it sounds like the people we already *got* in Washington. I'm Earl Pitts, American. Pitts Off.

Free Will

You know what makes me sick? You know what makes me so mad I just wanna drop my drawers... paint rings on my butt... an' let a Hell's Angels' biker bar use my keester for a dart board???

Yeah - I was down at the Duck Inn last night, twisting long-necks an' keeping the rabble in check. And my buddy Dub Meeker and Runt Wilson was in there... having one a' their legendary philosophical arguments. I'll tell you what - watching' these two brain-fighting about the universe is like watch Einstein and Freud going at it.

If - Einstein and Freud were the names of' two drunk monkeys.

Runt Wilson was making a point - and he needed back-up. So he goes... "Earl - what is the difference between your human... an' all your other animals?" He says – "I'll tell you what it is. It's free will. It's consciousness... the concept a' right an' wrong. It's the understanding of a higher power - and the free will to act on that."

Dub looked at me an' he goes... "Earl - I think it's the fact humans wipe."

I says - boys....those are both excellent points. Like that free will thing Runt's talking about.   I watch those animal shows on the cable. Every time a animal is doing something in nature... they're doing it on that "instinct". Spring gets here - the birds fly north... the bears wake up. They don't know how come - they just do it. That's cause the lord gave them instinct.

On the other hand... most of your animals feel no sense a' shame when it comes to pooping. They just let it go... in the middle of a field... down by the river... in the ocean... they don't care. It's like they don't even know it's happening sometimes. Bear's walking in the woods... plop!!! He did his daily dozen. Didn't need no toilet, no newspaper - no nothing.

An' Runt Wilson goes... "Well I appreciate the fact the Lord gave man free will. He gave us the ability to pursue our own interests based on our knowledge and our beliefs.

I looked at the bar and went... "And I appreciate the fact you boys ain't setting in here... "pooping on my floor."

Wake up, America. As far as the argument - I think they're both right. What sets your human apart from your other animals is free will... *and* your bowel control. An' maybe I would add opposable thumbs. Which is why animals can't eat sandwiches. I'm Earl Pitts, American. Pitts Off.

Redneck TV

You know what makes me sick? You know what makes me so mad I just wanna choke an' giraffe?

Me and the boys down at the Duck Inn made a sobering discovery last night. And trust me.. .when we're at the Duck Inn... anything that can sober us up... is some pretty heavy thinking.

We're not totally 110% sure on this... but me an' the boys down at the bar... might be the only genuine rednecks left in America... that don't have our own TV show. What the hell is going on?!?   You flip through your cable channels any night of the week - an' you'll find more rednecks than at dirt-track racing night at the county track.

So we were trying to figure out what kind of TV show we could do.   Runt Wilson said he ain't hunting alligators on account a' that's dangerous. He says - it's one thing to shoot an alligator - but apparently you have to catch them on a string an' pull them closer to you first.   That ain't red-neck... that's just stupid right there!

Dub Meeker said if we were rich an' made duck calls and we were all married to beautiful women... we could do a TV show..   Of course we ain't rich... we ain't got clue one how you make a duck call... and we ain't married to beautiful women. That's an 'Oh-fer' right there.

We could do our own version a' Hillbilly Hand-fishing... except the last time we tried that... we almost lost Runt Wilson's little brother Woodrow. That was the biggest dang catfish I ever saw, man! That sucker took Woodrow half ways across the lake... and along the bottom!! We swore off that sport. And now - probably that TV show.

We could do moon-shining'... or chopping down trees. But both of them involve work. We could dig for gold... or drive tracks across lakes. But those are both work, too. We just wanna get on TV - we don't want to actually have to *do* anything hard!

I could call my little boy Earl "Boo Boo" Junior... but that would be stupid. An' two stupid "Boo Boo" shows... is two stupid "Boo Boo" shows too many.

Wake up, America. All the good redneck TV show ideas is already took. Unless you like this one... "4x4... 2x4." We go off-roading in my truck... sneak up on animals... and hit them with pieces of lumber. And that sounds stupid - consider what we're up against. It's just crazy enough to be a hit. Watch for it... I'm Earl Pitts, American. Pitts Off.

Earl Pitts

Drinking Irresponsibly

You know what makes me sick? You know what makes me so mad I just wanna carve my initials... into the side of a grizzly bear... with my teeth?

Man... I got a big old case a' the goo-goo today. And I'm gonna take a stand... right here an' right now. And you people are my witness. Somebody write down the time.

Here's the deal. I want y'all to come down to the Duck Inn this week... to drink irresponsibly. That's right. I am tired of being told to drink responsibly. Bull-pucky!!!

You see a beer commercial... it says at the end, "drink responsibly". You see one a' those liquor ads... it says... "please drink responsibly".

Hey – you know what... you can all come down to the Duck Inn... an' drink *irresponsibly*. That's right. And you know why? Because your irresponsible drinkers... are a lot more interesting. An' I don't want "you know who" getting their panties all twisted. You know... your drunken driver mamas. I am not saying come to the Duck Inn... get polluted... and go jump in no car. I will insist you have a designated driver - or have your old lady come get you.

But once we get those details worked out... I don't care

what the hell you do. You can guzzle radiator fluid... if you think it'll give you a buzz. Bottoms up!

Can I just say... how boring would this world be -if everybody drank responsibly Most of your more interesting news stories feature irresponsible drinkers. Like if somebody accidentally blows something up... or catches himself on fire... or climbs into the lion pen at the zoo. And what do the police say? "Alcohol may have played a factor..." Dang straight it did!

The mamby-pamby, PC squirrels somehow got this whole country jacked up about drinking. They say you shouldn't drink to get drunk. You should only drink to take the edge off.

Well – I'm a redneck. I got a bigger edge than you do...

Wake up, America. I'm not going to lie to you - there are a lot of ugly drunks in this world. But there are just as many funny and entertaining ones. So come on down to the Duck Inn - and let's see where you fit in. Because in our place - alcohol *WILL* be a factor. I'm Earl Pitts, American. Pitts Off.

Earl Pitts

Looking Like Someone Famous

You know what makes me sick? You know what makes me so mad I just wanna wake up in the morning - and clean the sleep boogers out of my eyeballs... with the business end of a #2 pencil?

Now — has this ever happened to you? Has anybody ever told you that you look like somebody famous? Or maybe you saw somebody that looked like somebody famous – right? That's a rush, ain't it? You go... "Hey, you know who you look like?" And they go... "Yeah, George Clooney. I get that a lot..." An' then you go... "I was gonna say George *Lindsey*... but okay. It's your fantasy more than mine."

George Lindsey, a course... being TV's Goober. George Clooney... being a movie Goober.   They're easily confused for each other.

So I got a question... what if you see somebody that looks like a big star... but that star ain't human? In other words - should you mention it, if somebody looks like a cartoon?

Like the other day this guy comes in the Duck Inn... an' let me tell you something – the dude was a dead-ringer for Barney Rubble. I mean he had a giant head... blonde hair... no neck... an' arms so short he couldn't scratch his own rear-end if he wanted to.

Wake Up America!!!

Man… if he'd a' been wearing a tiger skin… an' came in there barefoot… I would have freaked out.   So – now do I tell this dude he looks like a cartoon? I mean, first of all - looking like Barney Rubble can't be that bad. Barney was a loyal friend to Fred Flintstone. His wife Betty was a knock-out. His little boy was incredibly strong. When you think about it - most of us probably wouldn't mind being Barney Rubble.

Anyway - me and my buddy, Dub Meeker were staring at this guy… an' he noticed. He goes, "What you looking at?" And Dub goes… "You know who you look like?" He kind of smiles and goes… "Yeah – I get that all the time. I look like that guy that played Barney Rubble in the Flintstones movies."

Okay – that's another way to look at it.

Wake up, America. Well – we all laughed about that - until his buddy come in there. Remember the cartoon Magilla Gorilla? Yeah – remember Mr. Peebles? What the hell is going on??? I'm Earl Pitts, American. Pitts Off.

Robbing a Redneck Bar

You know what makes me sick? You know what makes me so angry I just wanna have me a slap fight... with Edward Scissorhands?

Yeah – I met the two stupidest men on this whole dang planet last night. That would be these two nimrods that tried to rob the Duck Inn. I'll tell you what – those boys were desperate. Yeah – desperate for a butt-whuppin'. And they came to the right place.

See the thing was... those boys must have been from somewhere else. They didn't know what the Duck Inn was. Because nobody in their right mind robs a redneck bar. Not in no broad daylight. Hell Angel's are scared to go in a redneck bar.

I mean, don't get me wrong - redneck bars get hit all the time. But you just don't walk in and demand money, ya' fool. There's a certain way you gotta get money out of a redneck bar. Everybody knows it, too. Mostly... you climb up on the roof after hours... strip naked... slather on some lard all over your body... an' try to squeeze down the kitchen vent.

Wake Up America!!!

Now - I've never heard of that actually working. But that is the accepted norm in the criminal community.

But, see what happen last night was... I was twisting off long-necks... minding my own business. And all of a sudden – I'm looking at a knife. That sucker must have been two-foot long... right under my nose.

These two old boys were staring at me... all bug-eyed and crazy like. I mean, they were hepped up on crack, or meth, or horse tranquilizers or something. Because they were not exactly rational. The guy with the knife says... "Just give us your money, mister... and nobody has to get hurt".

I says... "Son... I don't want nobody to get hurt neither. But I can't control what happens from this point forward. You started it. If you come out of this shredded like the furniture in a cat-lady's house... it's your own dang fault."

Well – he runs that blade up under my Adam's apple... an' he goes... "You're the one with the knife at your neck, mister." An' I go... "An' you're the one with the .45 at your head... idiot."

Earl Pitts

Click. Right about then, Junior Meeker pulls out a Dirty Harry special about the size of a small howitzer. An' Junior goes – "Son... in three seconds, something's gonna hit this floor. It could be your knife. It could be your brains. It's up to you..."

Well – Evil Genius with the knife there - he's weighing his options. I didn't think he had that many options... he must have just been a slow thinker. Meanwhile, his buddy takes off like a cat with a sandpapered butt setting in turpentine... left a pee trail half ways out the front door.

I says... "I told you – it's your own fault".

So here's my advice for all you aspiring bad-actors an' evil-doers out there - Don't go trying to knock off a redneck bar. Start with something easier... like a mafia hang-out... or a biker bar. Somewhere where you *might* have a snowball's chance in hell of succeeding, I mean, you wanna take down a redneck bar... you got a better chance a' knocking off the cafeteria at the FBI.

Cause I don't care what kind of fire-power you bring in with you... you're gonna be out-manned... out-gunned... an' outta luck.

But I ain't gonna try scaring you with the fact we're gonna kill you. Because I know y'all are hepped up on

Wake Up America!!!

God knows what... an' maybe getting killed is a risk worth taking.

So... let me try to reason with you imbeciles. Like for instance... this is a redneck bar you boneheads! Everybody's drinking three-dollar longnecks... an' half of these losers are running tabs. We're not exactly flush with cash. So – unless your drug dealer's got a' Extra Value Menu... you ain't gonna get enough cash at a redneck bar to buy a bottle a' Tylenol.

Number two... I know you doped-up drug fiends are desperate people. And I respect that. But you haven't really seen desperate people... 'til you've been in a redneck bar. Every single guy in a redneck bar is carrying around a load a crap that makes your life look like zippidty-doo-dah. So you aren't exactly scaring us, Desperado. You're just rolling a lit road-flare into a room full a' dynamite.

Wake up, America. Number three... if there's one thing a redneck knows how to do... it's beating the crap out of somebody an' claimin' self-defense. When it really *IS* self-defense... lord, it's like Christmas come early. So if you boys would like a moment to rethink this...
I'm Earl Pitts, American. Pitts Off.

Earl Pitts

CHAPTER FIVE
WHAT REALLY MAKES ME SICK

Bible Thumpers

You know what makes me sick? You know what makes me so mad I just wanna go up to heaven... and rip the wings off angels...??

Yeah – that's pretty mad. But here's the deal... I had me another one of those evangelical
run-in's with those Bible thumpers again.

Yeah – I was home this weekend... by myself... when two Holy Rollers come pounding at my door. It was too late... they were standing right there by the screen door, looking right at me. So I couldn't exactly turn off the TV, lock the door an' hide under the window... like I usually do.

So I said to myself... you know what... maybe I should hear these boys out. I mean they look earnest. They certainly don't look dangerous. And' if they love the Lord enough to go door to door for him... who am I to dampen that passion for the scripture? I mean... why should I hide or run off people doing the Lord's work.

Either that... or I just felt like messing with them.

Anyway... I get to the door... and this clean-cut dude in a white shirt says, "Sir... can we take a few minutes of your time to talk to you about salvation." I says, "Son... I been waiting all day for somebody to talk to me about salvation." I says… "Come on in…" an' I threw open the screen door.

Well - those two boys looked at each other… like they just seen a naked lady. You know - they kind of lit up… but tried to play it cool.

They came in there… and I go, "Set down… on the couch. Let me get you boys something cool to drink." And I went in the kitchen an' got them both some ice water… I went back in the living room and I give each a' those boys a tall glass a water… to quench their thirst. And then I set back in my recliner… and I looked at them real serious and I go… "Now - what do you boys wanna talk to me about…?"

The older guy looked at the younger guy… and then he looked at me and he goes… "We're not sure. We never got this far…"

Wake up, America! I still don't know what those boys wanted to talk to me about. But they left two hours later… an' I think I got them coming to Baptist services on Sunday. I'm Earl Pitts, American. Pitts Off.

Employees of the Month

You know what makes me sick? You know what makes me so mad I just wanna go on disability... for tired brain? I mean – you can only think so much until your brain peters out.

You know who I hate? It's them goody-two-shoe, weasel, brown-nosing, suck-up, butt-kissers at work. And you know who you are. Of course... at work, they're not called brown-nosing, suck-up, butt-kissers. They're called... "Employees of the Month".

Yeah... me and the Meeker boys were down at the Duck Inn last night... giving old Runt Wilson hell on account of his brother Woodrow is the employee of the month down at the plant. Dub Meeker goes... "You know, none of us was ever employee of the month." And I go... "Yeah, how come we've been overlooked all these years?"

And Junior Meeker says... "Maybe it's because we get in there late every morning - and leave early every afternoon... screw around for eight hours... back-talk the bosses... waste materials... an' don't give a ding-darn about quality control. Plus we take way too many sick days... hot-rod the fork-lifts. And he looks at me and says... "And Earl... you did kind of harass the boss's daughter that one time..."

Earl Pitts

And Dub goes, "And I don't know how many times we got caught sneaking tools home in our lunch boxes. And there was more than once we got caught drinking in the parking lot during lunch." He says, "And Earl... you did threaten to punch-out that guy in the front office that time."

I'm thinking... and I go, "Naw...it's gotta be something else. I think what it is - they're discriminating against God-fearing, regular Real Americans. I think we hit the Redneck ceiling, boys."

Dub goes... "Earl, have you ever participated in trying to improve work?" I go, "Of course I have; remember back when they put in that new machine... an' it wasn't working? And they asked for suggestions what they could do with the machine..."

Dub goes... "You helped them fix that machine?"

I go, "No... but I did make a suggestion what they could do with it..."

Wake up, America. So listen up... you suck-up Employees of the Month . You get to park closer to the door for the month – big deal. Your lips are just that much closer to the boss's butt, too. Not interested. I'm Earl Pitts, American. Pitts Off.

Making Children Wimps

You know what makes me sick? You know what makes me so mad I just wanna travel the globe searching for the fattest man on earth - and then ask him if he'll teeter-totter with me.

Yeah - once again... we're going out of our way to make our kids into wimps. That's what we do anymore, you know. Lord, we handle them like they was diamonds. They're so precious... so fragile. I say - Bull-puckey!!!

I heard this story... some school district in West Virginia took out all the swing sets on their playgrounds. On account of some little girl jumped off a swing last year and broke her arm. And of course - her parents sued the school. So the new rule is no swing sets... for no kids... no at time.

You know - maybe for recess... instead of getting their coats on... we could wrap every little kid with bubble-wrap an' then send them outside.

Now – when I was a kid, your standard American playground was basically your obstacle course of death. There wasn't one piece of equipment on the playground that couldn't kill you.

We had swing sets. An' yes - they can be dangerous.

Earl Pitts

But not the swinging part. It was dangerous what we did. We'd let the other kids swing... and we'd run through the middle - trying to time it so we didn't get kicked half ways to Kingdom Come. I mean, you take a fifth-grader in the face... you'll feel that for a while.

Then there's your teeter-totter. That can be an innocent and fulfilling experience. It can also be deathly boring. That's why we turned the teeter-totter into a six-year old's Junior Astronaut launch pad. If your butt never flipped over the handles... an' you landed *behind* the guy on the other side... you weren't doing it right.

We had a merry-go-round. We called it... *the vomit comet*. You get all the queasy girls on there... and spin it so hard they either spit up... or fly off into the gravel. Yeah – what does an' eight year old know about centrifugal force? Nothin'

And of course my favorites... were always the jungle gym and the monkey bars. I'll tell you how much I loved those puppies - I dislocated my shoulder two times in fifth grade. And my mama never sued nobody. What did we used to call it back then? Oh yeah - it was a part of *growing up!!!*

Wake up, America. Yeah, we'd get done with recess... there'd be so much blood on the ground... it looked like a Mexican border town. And somehow - we survived. Well – most of us. I'm Earl Pitts, American. Pitts Off.

Tag-less Underpants, Really!??!?

You know what makes me sick? You know what makes me so mad I just wanna step in and try to break up a fight between a badger an' a bobcat?

I have warned y'all repeatedly about the wussification of the American male. Your all-American, red-blooded, hard-workin' male of the species is now about as rare as left-overs at Honey Boo Boo's house.

Women have done everything they could to chick us up... "girl-ify" us... if you will. They have systematically stripped away everything that makes us men.

Here is just the latest example of what I'm talking 'bout. What do you think is the number one concern of men today? What is the number one thing on every man's mind...the thing that's got him most worried. Well - according to the commercials I've been watching... it's underwear tags.

What!!??! Used to be... you wanted to make a man happy... you bought him a new gun rack for his truck... or a new trolling motor for his bass boat. You want to impress a man today? You buy him underpants without tags!!

These commercials go... tag-less underpants don't

scratch - they don't itch. Let me ask you a question... are you a real man... or are you the Princess an' the Pea?? I mean - holy smokes... if a real man finds a good pair of shorts that keeps his equipment sheltered with room, comfort an' support... he doesn't care if the waist band is made out sand paper!! Or at least - he shouldn't!

And you know who they've got sellin' tag-less underpants? Michael Jordan!!! The greatest basketball player of all time... turns out to be the biggest wuss of all time, too!! Yeah - when Michael Jordan goes all sensitive an' turns girl on us... what chance do the rest of us have???

Wake up, America! An' by the way Michael... you try to tear the tag off my underpants... you're gonna pull back a bloody stump, son. I don't need your hands back there. That's creepy. I'm Earl Pitts, American. Pitts Off.

Whatever Happened to White Walls

You know what makes me sick? You know what makes me so angry I just wanna volunteer down at the zoo... to give out the elephant enemas?

Yeah – y'all know the problem with old cars? Trying to get them fixed! Like my old lady... she's got an '89 Escort... still runs like the day we brought it home. Course – the day we brought it home – it ran like crap. That being said - the car's got one thing going for it - it's paid for!

Anyway – she got a flat tire a couple days ago. Have you ever looked for a tire for a '89 Escort? You'd have better luck looking for gold bars and unicorn fur - up your butt! I went down to the tire store... and told guy behind the counter I needed a tire for a '89 Escort. He says – "do I want a performance tire... a' all-weather tire... or a' touring tire. I told him - I wanted a' inflated tire".

He goes, "What kind of rims you got on there?" Escort rims. This is when I find out - apparently buying tires for a '89 Escort is a little like buying wheels for your covered wagon. He pulls out these giant books from all over the place... he's checking out numbers... cross-referencing lord knows what. He says he thinks he's got something I can use.

Earl Pitts

Then I threw him. I go... "You got that in a white wall?" He looked at me like I just started talking in Wookie. He goes, "What the hell's a white wall? Is that a brand?"

Now maybe I'm getting' way too old... or maybe I was just dreaming... but didn't we used to paint the sides of our tires white? Whatever happened to that? That was a good look. I remember you used to pay a little more for a white stripe on your tire. Then you could drive around looking like some stuck-up, hoity-toity swell. I mean, you might not have been driving a Cadillac. But for ten bucks a pop - you could be driving on the same tires.

He says... "they don't have white walls". He says, "nobody has white walls... except for maybe down at the junk yard". And he goes – "you still want the tires". She'll just drive around on that hard-rubber spare... until white walls come back in fashion.

At this point, he's rolling his eyes a lot and just wants to get me out of the store. He goes, "Well, is there anything else you need?" I says, "Yeah - do you carry vinyl top wax?"

Wake up, America! I get home and I tell my old lady I got good news and bad news. The bad news... they don't got the stuff we need to fix her car. The good news... she apparently owns a classic. I'm Earl Pitts, American. Pitts Off.

Organic Food

You know what makes me sick? You know what makes me so mad I just wanna eat a pine cone? Not for the natural, organic benefits... just so I could enjoy passing it!!!

Yeah – there's only one group a' people I hate more than your squirrel-hugging PETA nitwits... and those dope-smoking, electric-car driving, Yuppie green environmental weenies...

That's right - it's your self-righteous, blow-hard organic boneheads.

You see these twisted old burned-out hippies in the grocery store all the time. They're hunting out the "organic" food because it's better for them. Organic milk... organic cheese... organic vegetables.

Hey – you know what's organic? Dirt. Why don't you chew on some dirt – you earth-shoe wearing numbskulls!!!??

Yeah – they did this big study over in England somewhere... and they found out organic food ain't no better for you than regular food. However, it does cost more.

An' I know you VW-bus driving love-children of

Earl Pitts

Woodstock are out there is saying... "But Earl... Organic food has no pesticides." Do you people even listen to yourselves sometimes??

Do you know who has to be worried about eating pesticides? Bugs!

So unless you belong to a secret society of bug-people... you ain't got nothing to worry about.

Like I seen these organic eggs at the store. Six organic eggs - were five bucks! Now – a dozen regular eggs...I s about half that. That's two times the eggs... for half the price. Do the math. For those prices... I don't care if my chicken is hepped up on crack, heroin... steroids... Flomax... or those drops for excessive dry eye... it's a stinking *EGG* for crying out loud!!!

Here's another one you organic goobers keep throwing at us - You like your chickens to "free-range". You don't like it when your bucket of fried chicken has been kept in little cages and stuffed with hormones. So they just wander anywhere they want and scratch the ground to survive.

Yeah – in humans, we call that – vagrants. Do you think a homeless bum is healthier than somebody got a home???

Wake up, America! Organic food has no pesticides... no

Wake Up America!!!

hormones… no steroids… and no chemicals. Generally bought by people with no brains…an' no common sense… I'm Earl Pitts, American. Pitts off!!!

Earl Pitts

Toilet Paper Conspiracy

You know what makes me sick? You know what makes me so mad I just wanna go back in time... and slap a Pilgrim?

Man, this is making me crazier than a baboon with hemorrhoids. An' this is it... Toilet paper.

What got me thinking about this... I heard this story where they're coming out with special toilet paper for little kids. What they call a "toilet paper system". It's supposed to teach little kids how to use the bathroom. What they do is put little dog paw prints on four sheets... and a picture of a puppy on the fifth... to teach little kids where to tear and how much to use.

My question is... do they have something clever like that - to teach my *family*?

Man, these free-loaders in my house go through toilet paper like grizzly bears go through salmon. Don't worry about me squeezing the Charmin... hell I can't even *find* it anymore. I mean, I always figured we were a regular American family. I just didn't know we were *that* regular.

Now – see if you agree with me on this here. It's partly because my family doesn't have the self-control... or the puppy paw toilet paper to train with. And it's partly a toilet paper conspiracy. I swear - they're not putting as much paper on the rolls as they used to.

I mean, remember when we were kids? You never ran out of toilet paper. Your mama would go to the store and buy a two-pack... and that would last a family of six... for a year! And we *still* had enough left over to TP houses on Halloween. At least that's the way I remember it.

Nowadays... you buy one of those Wal*Mart packages - I think it has 314 rolls of toilet paper inside. And that's good for a couple weeks. If you're lucky and nobody ate something bad. Because if there's a bug running through your kids - you'll probably end up using Bounty towels before it's all over.

Wake up, America! Now – I'm not saying the disappearing toilet paper this is the biggest problem facing the country today – that would be terrorism. But this is definitely the number two problem. I'm Earl Pitts, American. Pitts Off.

Dying at Home

You know what makes me sick? You know what makes me so mad I just wanna go to an Exorcists' garage sale... and buy up all their old Ouija boards?

Yeah - I heard this story the other day... they was saying more people are trying to die at home these day. And of course - I mean among people that are dying anyway. It's not some kind of spur of the moment thing.

I found out - it's true. Ten years ago... more people died in the hospital. Now, people like to go home to die. They want to be surrounded by family and friends in a familiar place... close to the heart.

Now - that's a beautiful thing. *Unless* you're the family member that gets that room after they're dead and toted out. *That's* gonna wake you up in the middle of the night a couple times a week.

Now, this fact doesn't mean much to me because I come from a long line of men that keeled over at work. Pitts men not only work until we drop over... we got a long history of dropping over *AT* work.

But that being said... if I had my druthers... I would like die in a hospital.

Wake Up America!!!

Number one - if I'm old enough an' I die at home... there's a good chance my old lady wouldn't tell anybody an' keeps collecting my social security checks. I don't want my grandkids finding Grandpa's mummified remains in the bedroom closet when they come over for Thanksgiving. That could stunt a younger child's mental development for quite some time.

Number two - hospitals are generally better equipped to help you *NOT* die. Just about the time I flat-line... I'd like to see a team a' professionals in white coats and a crash cart rushing through the door... instead of my old lady and little boy coming in with a car battery and jumper cables.

Number three - once you are dead... hospitals are a lot more used to dealing with it. I would like to die in the hands of professionals. I'd hate for my old lady to think I was dead... and have to call the neighbor over for a second opinion.

Wake up, America! Yeah - I'd hate to have my wife and the neighbor - lady Naomi poking me with a stick half the night - to see if I was really dead. I'd like them to desist on the deceased. I'm Earl Pitts, American. Pitts Off.

Apologies

You know what makes me sick? You know what makes me so mad I just wanna French-kiss... a snappin' turtle?

Yeah – more research out there. You know, these pencil-necked science dweebs are working overtime just to find out stuff the rest of us won't believe.

Get this latest piece of hog-wash. They say women apologize more than men. Uh huh - obviously they skipped over *MY* house doing their research. Yeah – they said it wasn't because men don't *want* to apologize when we screw up - it's just men have a higher threshold of what we think deserves an apology.

I've got news for these four-eyed, twisted nut-balls. It doesn't have anything to do with what us men think deserves an apology.   It's about what our old ladies think deserves an apology.

I remember one time... I took my old lady to the Walmart. Well, she was doing whatever it is she does there... which is mostly going crazy and burning through my cash. And I'm bent over the cart you know... kind of zoned out. Suddenly - she whups me upside the head. I go, "What the heck was that for?!?!" She goes... "I saw you looking at that woman over there... you pig!!" I go,

Wake Up America!!!

"What woman?!? I was daydreaming!" An' she goes... "You are so pathetic..."

Number one... if I was going to go looking at women... would I hang out at the Walmart? Hell no. I'd take her shopping to the Victoria's Secret store.

So here's the deal. My old lady wouldn't talk to me for three days until I apologized for staring at a woman I wasn't even staring at!!! An' this goes on all the time. She got mad at me one time - for what she said I was *thinking!*

On the other hand - does she ever apologize to me? Hell no. Because everything she does wrong... is somehow my fault! Like last week... I'm mad as a hornet... and I go... "Pearl, why in the blue blazes did you back into the mail-box? Are you blind?" And she goes... "Because I told you to move that mail-box to the other side of the driveway... two years ago!!"

I go... "Don't you know how to back up a car?" And she goes... "Didn't I tell you not to put those Dale Junior decals on the back window? How am I supposed to see?!"

That's right - it's my fault she can't drive. So I had to apologize to her - for her hitting the mailbox. Does this sound familiar men?

Earl Pitts

Wake up, America! Yeah – this study said women apologize more than men. My question is - in which alternative universe did they conduct this study? I'm Earl Pitts, American. Pitts Off.

ABOUT THE AUTHOR

Earl Pitts, American has been entertaining hundreds of thousands of people daily with his legendary commentaries heard on radio stations across the country since 1985.   .

For the most part - he's just like you. (That is - if you entertained hundreds of thousands of people daily with radio commentaries.) He works in a factory by day... and picks up shifts at The Duck Inn Bar at night to make ends meet. Meanwhile - his family – wife, Pearl and kids, Earl Junior and Sandra Dee keep pushing his ends farther apart. (Wow - except for that radio thing - this is your life!).

Earl's buddies, Dub and Junior Meeker, and Runt Wilson will never be mistaken for MENSA members. In fact - they probably couldn't even spell "MENSA". Earl's 14-year old son is getting over a break-up after a two year relationship with his teacher... and Earl's daughter has been in her room crying for the last three years after Homeland Security arrested her fiancé in the middle of their wedding.

And what can you say about Earl's wife Pearl? Some people hit the lottery in life - and find the perfect life companion, an extension of their own soul. Others marry people like Pearl. Enough said.

In other words - it's your typical American life. And it all contributes to Earl's unique take on the world.

Made in the USA
Lexington, KY
05 March 2014